C29 0000 0809 796

KV-577-014

THE WORLD OF ARTIFICIAL INTELLIGENCE

ARTIFICIAL INTELLIGENCE
AND HUMANOID ROBOTS

BY ALICIA Z. KLEPEIS

raintree

a Capstone company — publishers for children

Raintree is an imprint of Capstone Global Library Limited, a company incorporated in England and Wales having its registered office at 264 Banbury Road, Oxford, OX2 7DY – Registered company number: 6695582

www.raintree.co.uk
myorders@raintree.co.uk

Text © Capstone Global Library Limited 2020
The moral rights of the proprietor have been asserted.

All rights reserved. No part of this publication may be reproduced in any form or by any means (including photocopying or storing it in any medium by electronic means and whether or not transiently or incidentally to some other use of this publication) without the written permission of the copyright owner, except in accordance with the provisions of the Copyright, Designs and Patents Act 1988 or under the terms of a licence issued by the Copyright Licensing Agency, Barnard's Inn, 86 Fetter Lane, London, EC4A 1EN (www.cla.co.uk). Applications for the copyright owner's written permission should be addressed to the publisher.

Edited by Karen Aleo and Christopher Harbo
Designed by Brann Garvey
Original illustrations © Capstone Global Library Limited 2020
Picture research by Pam Mitsakos and Tracy Cummins
Production by Kathy McColley
Originated by Capstone Global Library Ltd
Printed and bound in India

ISBN 978 1 4747 8178 7 (hardcover)   ISBN 978 1 4747 7104 7 (paperback)
23 22 21 20 19   23 22 21 20 19
10 9 8 7 6 5 4 3 2 1   10 9 8 7 6 5 4 3 2 1

British Library Cataloguing in Publication Data
A full catalogue record for this book is available from the British Library.

Acknowledgements
We would like to thank the following for permission to reproduce photographs: Getty Images: AFP/WILLIAM WEST, 7, Bloomberg/Kiyoshi Ota, 26-27, Iconica/Peter Cade, 12-13, Matt Cardy, 28-29, The Christian Science Monitor/Ann Hermes, 18-19; Newscom: dpa/picture-alliance/Peter Forster, 22-23, REUTERS/KIM HONG-JI, 10, Xinhua News Agency/Chen Zixia, 4-5; Science Source/NYPL, 9; Shutterstock: Everett Historical, 6, Attila JANDI, 20, catwalker, 11, MikeDotta 15, 24-25, Ociacia, Cover, Sarunyu L., 21, Supphachai Salaeman, Design Element; The Image Works: Fujifotos/Tatsuyuki Tayama, 16-17. The publisher does not endorse products whose logos may appear on objects in images in this book.

Every effort has been made to contact copyright holders of material reproduced in this book. Any omissions will be rectified in subsequent printings if notice is given to the publisher.

All the internet addresses (URLs) given in this book were valid at the time of going to press. However, due to the dynamic nature of the internet, some addresses may have changed, or sites may have changed or ceased to exist since publication. While the author and publisher regret any inconvenience this may cause readers, no responsibility for any such changes can be accepted by either the author or the publisher.

CONTENTS

A WORLD OF ROBOTS

Oh no! You're on holiday with your family when you realize that you've left your toothbrush at home. What are you going to do? You quickly call the hotel reception to see if they can help. Three minutes later, you hear a knock at the door. You open it to find a robotic butler holding a new toothbrush!

Later that day, your family isn't sure where to eat dinner. You whip out your smartphone and ask it for options. A digital assistant quickly gives you three choices. You could choose the fast food place where robots cook the burgers. Or you could go to the cafe where a robot makes the coffee. Instead your family decides on a restaurant where robot waiters serve your meal.

FACT

The word robot comes from a 1920 Czech play, *Rossum's Universal Robots*, about mechanical workers called *robota*.

Does this holiday seem like pure fantasy? It's not! Recent advances in **humanoid** robots and artificial intelligence (AI) are making all of these things possible.

Robot waiters already serve food at some restaurants in China.

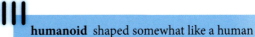

humanoid shaped somewhat like a human

CHAPTER 1

RISE OF THE HUMANOID ROBOTS

The history of humanoid robots goes back much further than you might think. The earliest robots just followed commands from humans. But as technology improved, these machines became smarter with the help of artificial intelligence.

EARLY HUMANOID ROBOTS

People began dreaming about robots long before they could build them. In the 400s BC, a Chinese **philosopher** called Lie Yukou wrote about an **automaton**. This human-like machine was described as being able to move its head, walk and even sing.

By the 1490s, inventor and artist Leonardo da Vinci actually drew plans for a humanoid robot. Da Vinci never built the robot. But he imagined a series of pulleys and cables that would allow it to walk, move its head and wave.

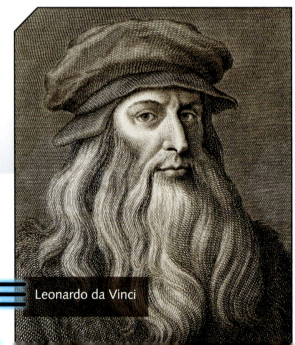

Leonardo da Vinci

Roughly 280 years later, a French watchmaker called Pierre Jaquet-Droz built several working automatons. One of them was called The Writer. This clockwork machine had more than 6,000 parts, including gears and springs. It could blink its eyes and move its head. Most amazingly, The Writer could be programmed to write messages up to 40 letters long. And between words, it dipped a **quill** into an inkwell!

FACT

Da Vinci never built his robot, but others have. A 2009 exhibition in Melbourne, Australia, featured a life-size recreation of it based on his drawings.

philosopher person who studies ideas and the way people think, and who searches for knowledge

automaton machine that looks and moves like a human or an animal

quill pen made from a bird's feather

HUMANOID ROBOTS OF THE 1900s

The 1900s saw giant leaps in robotics and humanoid robots. In 1939 a robot called Elektro amazed people at the World's Fair in New York, USA. This 2-metre- (7-foot-) tall voice-controlled robot walked, talked and made jokes. Elektro could even blow up balloons.

In 1957 an Italian engineer built a robot called Cygan. The 2.4-metre- (8-foot-) tall giant was made of 300,000 parts. Controlled remotely, Cygan could shuffle forwards and backwards. It could also move its arms and crush cans with its hands.

In the early 1970s, artificial intelligence started to appear in humanoid robots when Japanese engineers built WABOT-1. This high-tech humanoid robot could measure distances and directions to objects. It also had hands that could grip and move objects. WABOT-1 could even talk to people in Japanese.

FACT
Japan is a leader in robotics. It makes more than half of the world's robots.

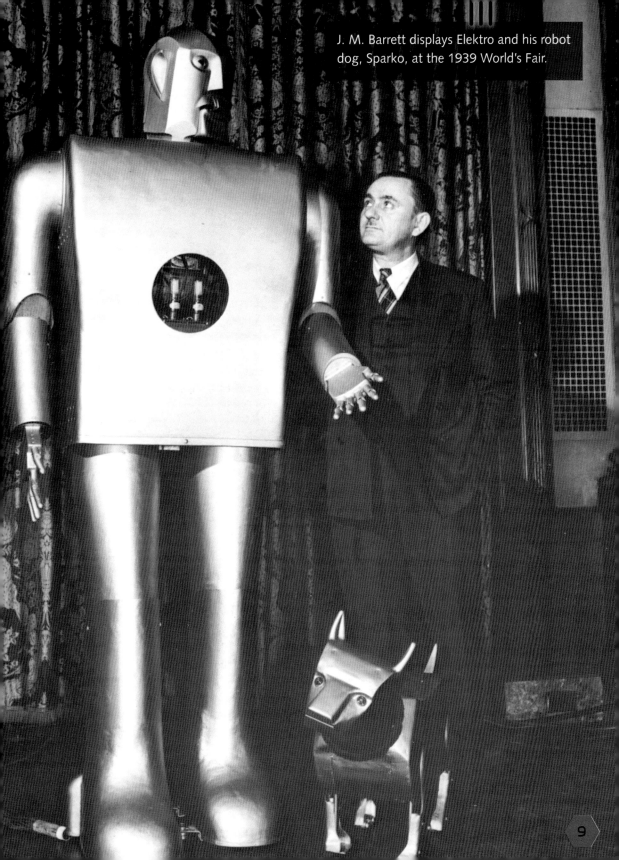

21ST CENTURY HUMANOID ROBOTS

Human robot research is advancing much more quickly in the 21st century. In 2000, Honda introduced ASIMO. This two-legged robot's AI programming allows it to walk in many directions and even go up and down stairs. ASIMO can also detect moving objects and recognize human hand motions.

Honda isn't the only company developing humanoid robots that use AI. Boston Dynamics' Atlas robot can do more than just walk. It can lift heavy boxes, jump onto platforms and even stand back up after it falls down. Designed for dangerous military missions and emergencies, Atlas may one day help to save lives.

FACT

The very first robot skiing tournament took place near the 2018 Winter Olympics in South Korea.

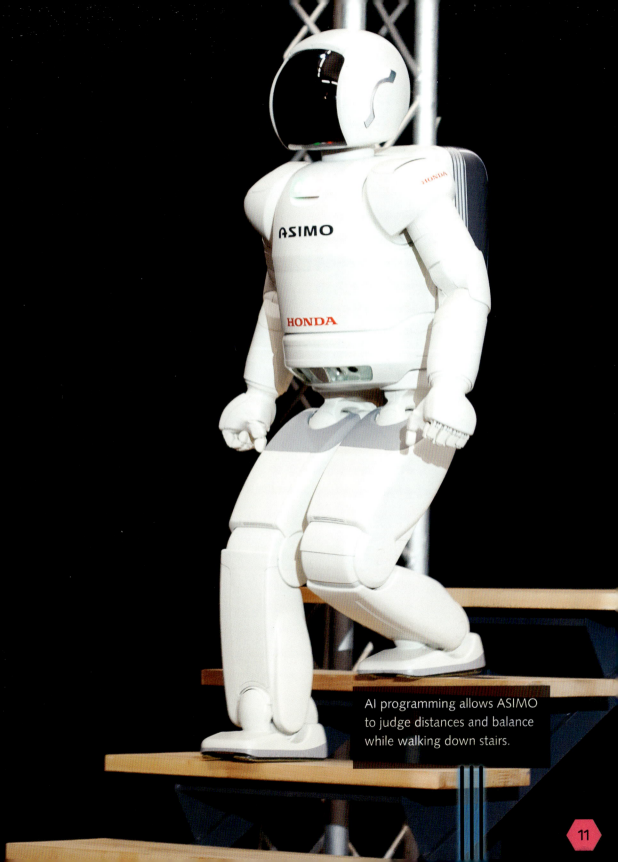

AI programming allows ASIMO to judge distances and balance while walking down stairs.

CHAPTER 2

HUMANOID ROBOTS IN ACTION

People often talk about **robots** learning new things. But most robots don't really learn on their own. Computer programmers and engineers must tell robots what to do and how to do it. They design software that gives robots very clear directions.

UNDERSTANDING ALGORITHMS

Scientists and engineers use **algorithms** to help robots work. An algorithm is a detailed set of directions to complete a task or solve a problem. Although you might not realize it, algorithms are more common than you think. For instance, a recipe for chocolate chip cookies is a type of algorithm. So are the directions for folding a jumper.

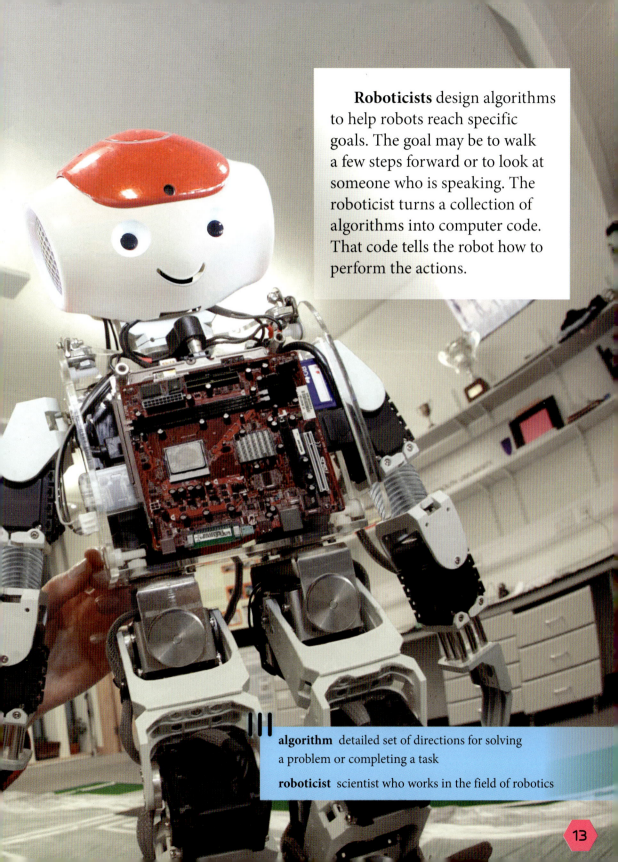

Roboticists design algorithms to help robots reach specific goals. The goal may be to walk a few steps forward or to look at someone who is speaking. The roboticist turns a collection of algorithms into computer code. That code tells the robot how to perform the actions.

algorithm detailed set of directions for solving a problem or completing a task

roboticist scientist who works in the field of robotics

ADDING AI

Scientists are now trying to train robots to learn on their own. They are working on code that will give robots artificial intelligence. AI allows machines to solve problems and do tasks that usually require human intelligence.

For humanoid robots, artificial intelligence allows them to learn by watching someone else. For instance, a robot with AI watching someone pick up an object could learn the best way to grasp that object. When it's the robot's turn to pick up the object, whether it's a pencil or a cup, the robot will do it correctly. Over time the robot may even come up with new ways to complete the task on its own.

THE TURING TEST

In 1950, a computer scientist called Alan Turing developed the Turing Test. It tested if people could tell the difference between machine behaviours and human behaviours. If someone couldn't tell if a behaviour was from a machine or a human, the machine passed the test. Today, the Turing Test is a key part of the philosophy of artificial intelligence.

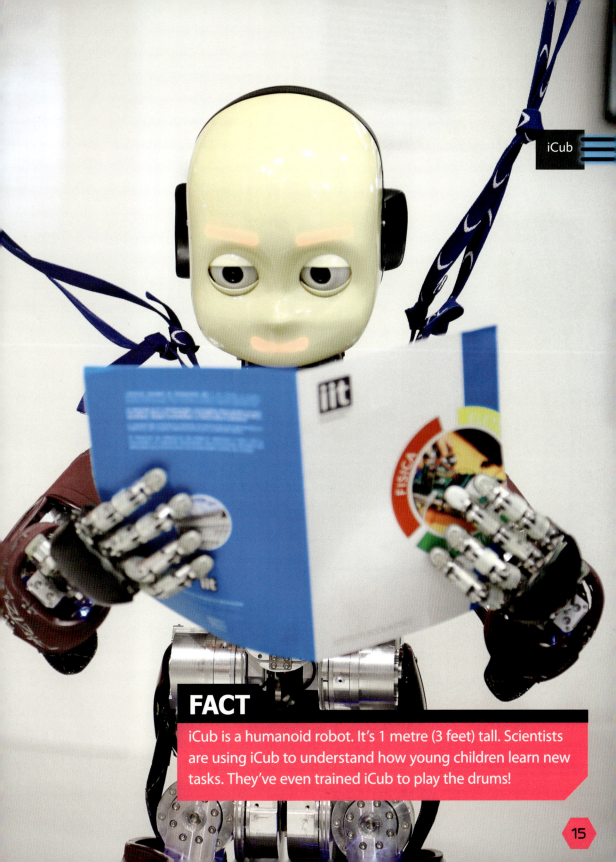

iCub

FACT

iCub is a humanoid robot. It's 1 metre (3 feet) tall. Scientists are using iCub to understand how young children learn new tasks. They've even trained iCub to play the drums!

15

SENSING THE WORLD

Every day we use our senses to experience the world. Robots can be programmed to see, hear and touch things too.

ASIMO uses its sense of touch to give and receive objects.

Humanoid robots see and hear with the help of cameras and microphones. For example, Honda's ASIMO robot has two cameras in its head. It uses them to see and map its surrounding area. When an object blocks its path, ASIMO can see it and avoid it while still moving forward. The robot also has microphones that help it to pick up sounds and recognize voices.

ASIMO has force **sensors** to detect when it touches things. The robot uses its sense of touch to pick up objects and shake hands. ASIMO can even move backwards or forwards when its hand is pushed or pulled.

Roboticists are constantly working to improve the sense of touch in robots. More advanced sensors help robots know how much force to apply to something they're holding. For instance, a robot picking up an egg needs to know that too much force will crush it.

sensor device that measures a physical property such as temperature or brightness

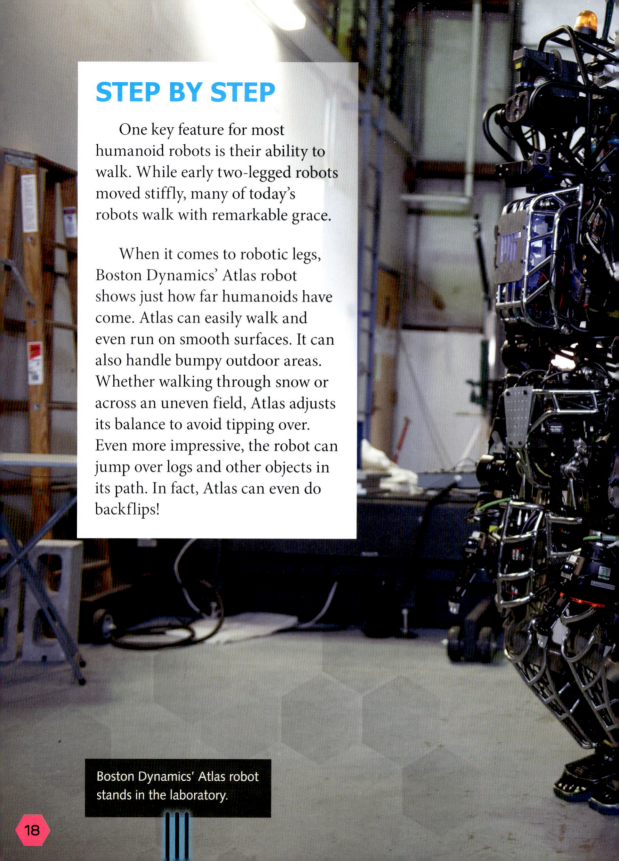

STEP BY STEP

One key feature for most humanoid robots is their ability to walk. While early two-legged robots moved stiffly, many of today's robots walk with remarkable grace.

When it comes to robotic legs, Boston Dynamics' Atlas robot shows just how far humanoids have come. Atlas can easily walk and even run on smooth surfaces. It can also handle bumpy outdoor areas. Whether walking through snow or across an uneven field, Atlas adjusts its balance to avoid tipping over. Even more impressive, the robot can jump over logs and other objects in its path. In fact, Atlas can even do backflips!

Boston Dynamics' Atlas robot stands in the laboratory.

KENGORO

Kengoro is a humanoid robot from Japan. It can do press-ups, pull-ups and backbends. To move its arms and legs, Kengoro's **actuators** pull wires in a similar way to human muscles when they contract. These actuators produce heat. Kengoro appears to sweat, thanks to tubes of water throughout the robot. But the sweat isn't just for looks. It's part of the robot's cooling system. Kengoro could burn out its motors without it.

actuator mechanical device for moving or controlling something

CHAPTER 3

AMAZING ADVANCES

Walking well and sensing the world around them are important advances for humanoid robots. But many modern robots can do so much more. From talking to people to understanding human emotions, AI is taking humanoid robots to new heights.

TALKING ROBOTS

Today many humanoid robots can speak. Some even have jobs where they talk to customers. Otonaroid is a communications **android** that looks very much like a Japanese woman. It works at a museum in Tokyo. It talks directly to museum visitors. How does this robot talk? It moves its lips to match speech that's been pre-recorded. Otonaroid can also show different facial expressions.

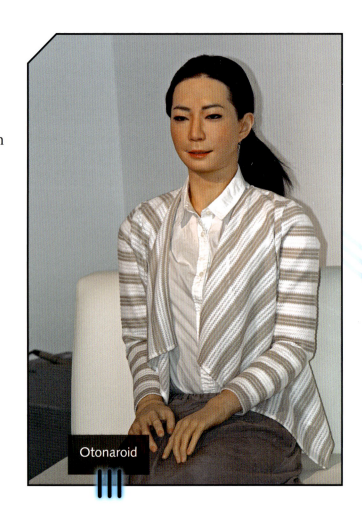

Otonaroid

Kirobo Mini

Talking humanoid robots have even been put to work in space. In 2013, Japan sent Kirobo to the International Space Station. This 33-centimetre- (13-inch-) tall robot spoke Japanese and was designed to keep astronauts company in space. After Kirobo's 18-month mission, the car company Toyota developed a mini version of the robot that stands only 10 centimetres (4 inches) tall.

In the near future, talking robots might work as receptionists in offices. They may even help guide people who are visiting large shopping centres.

FACT

A humanoid robot called Sophia can answer interview questions. AI allows it to respond to questions, make eye contact and show emotions.

android robot that looks very similar to a human being

ROBOTS WITH SPECIAL TALENTS

Many humanoid robots walk and talk. But others have special skills. In the 1980s, the Japanese robot WABOT-2 could play an electric keyboard. Today robots have been designed and programmed to play the trumpet, violin, guitar and more.

A robotic head created in Taiwan can read and perform music. It uses cameras and an algorithm to read sheet music in about 40 seconds. Then it sends that information through a voice **synthesizer** to sing a song.

What else can humanoid robots read? The news! A lifelike android called Erica may one day replace a human newsreader in Japan. Erica can read scripted writing out loud and hold conversations with people. Her creator hopes that one day Erica will be able to think and act on her own.

FACT

Motobot 2.0 is a robot motorcycle rider that can race around a track at 200 kilometres (124 miles) per hour!

synthesizer electronic instrument that makes a wide variety of sounds by creating and combining signals of different frequencies

ROBOTS PLAY FOOTBALL

Players speed down the football pitch. They pass the ball from player to player. Pass, shoot . . . goal! All players in the RoboCup football tournament are robots. Playing football has many AI challenges. One is walking quickly and, one day, running. Another is seeing the ball on the pitch. And then there's working with other members of the team. The founders of the RoboCup competition have a goal for this project. They want robot players to beat human World Cup champions by the year 2050.

ROBOTS AND EMOTIONS

When we talk to other people we also share our emotions. Doing so helps us to understand how others feel and builds connections. Could robots build connections with people if they understood emotions too? Some scientists think so. They have designed humanoid robots that can respond to our emotions.

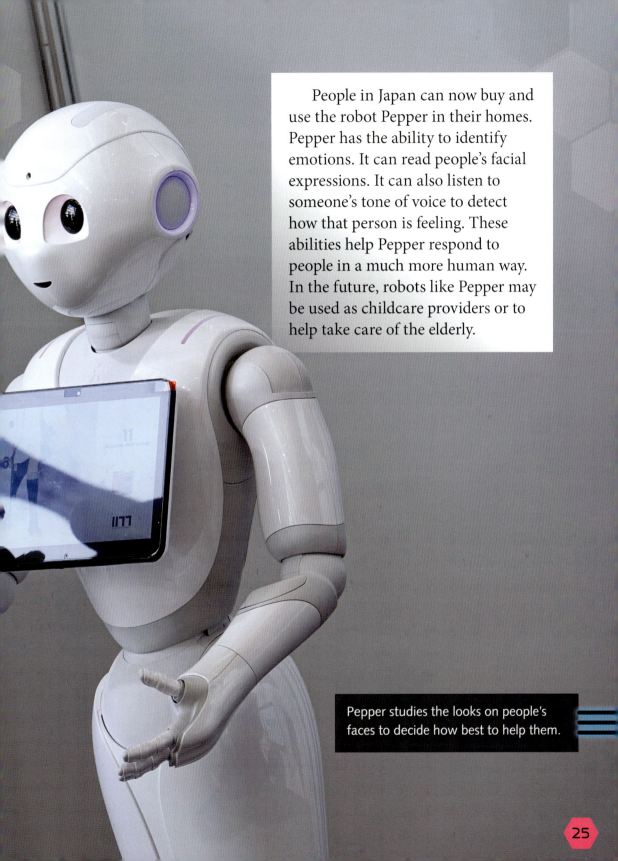

People in Japan can now buy and use the robot Pepper in their homes. Pepper has the ability to identify emotions. It can read people's facial expressions. It can also listen to someone's tone of voice to detect how that person is feeling. These abilities help Pepper respond to people in a much more human way. In the future, robots like Pepper may be used as childcare providers or to help take care of the elderly.

Pepper studies the looks on people's faces to decide how best to help them.

ROBOT OR HUMAN?

Humanoid technology has improved so much it's hard to tell if some robots are machines or real people. One such example is Actroid. Modelled on a young Japanese woman, this robot can blink and appear to breathe. Its **silicone** skin looks like a real person's skin.

A newer Actroid robot, Actroid-SIT, is even more realistic. It can work **autonomously** to react to changes in its surroundings. This feature allows Actroid-SIT to talk to groups of people and make eye contact. The robot can also handle interruptions and smoothly switch from one topic to the next. Not only that, Actroid-SIT can point and wave to show it is paying attention.

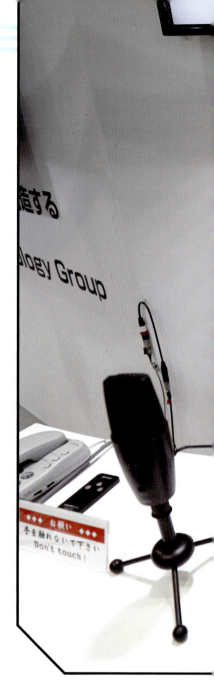

FACT

In 2015 an android actress known as Geminoid F starred in the Japanese film *Sayonara*.

© Kyoei Sangyo Co.,Ltd.

An Actroid humanoid robot at an exhibition in Tokyo, Japan, awaits a chance to speak directly to customers.

silicone material that is resistant to water and high temperatures, and can be rubbery

autonomous having the ability to carry out a job on one's own; autonomous robots are not operated remotely by a person

CHAPTER 4

LOOKING TO THE FUTURE

With humanoid robots becoming more advanced every year, what does the future hold? Will human workers find themselves out of jobs as robots replace them? Will robots always treat everyone with kindness and compassion? Could humanoid robots one day take over the world the way they do in some films?

We don't know the answers to these questions yet. But it's important to remember that artificial intelligence and humanoid robots are tools. Robots may take over some jobs that people find dangerous or repetitive. But these robots may also create a demand for new jobs in different fields such as robotics and computer engineering. People will need to know how to maintain and repair the robots.

No matter what, roboticists need to make sure artificial intelligence and robotics remain **ethical** and fair in the future. Robots must be programmed to help people and treat everyone equally. And when this happens, it will be exciting to see what future humanoid robots will do.

ethical having to do with beliefs about right and wrong behaviour

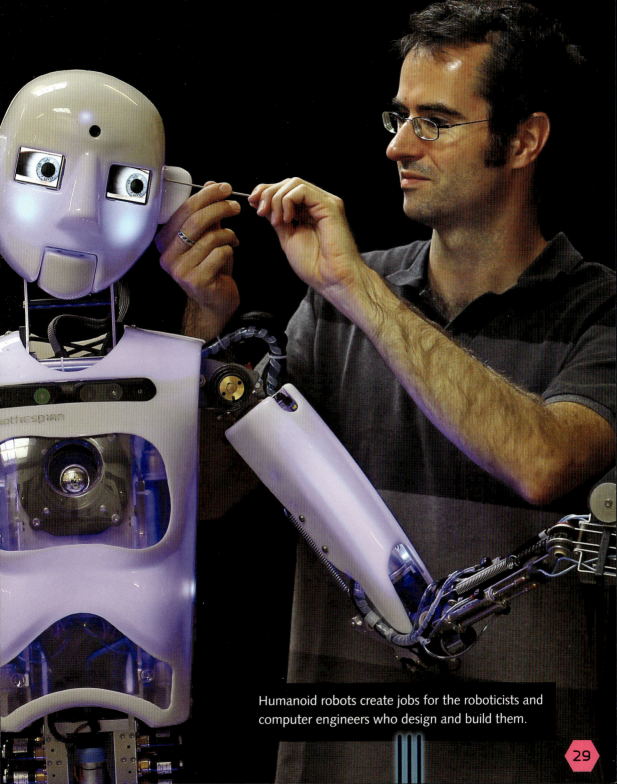

Humanoid robots create jobs for the roboticists and computer engineers who design and build them.

GLOSSARY

actuator mechanical device for moving or controlling something

algorithm detailed set of directions for solving a problem or completing a task

android robot that looks very similar to a human being

automaton machine that looks and moves like a human or an animal

autonomous having the ability to carry out a job on one's own; autonomous robots are not operated remotely by a person

ethical having to do with beliefs about right and wrong behaviour

humanoid shaped somewhat like a human

philosopher person who studies ideas and the way people think, and who searches for knowledge

quill pen made from a bird's feather

roboticist scientist who works in the field of robotics

sensor device that measures a physical property such as temperature or brightness

silicone material that is resistant to water and high temperatures, and can be rubbery

synthesizer electronic instrument that makes a wide variety of sounds by creating and combining signals of **different frequencies**

FIND OUT MORE

BOOKS

Computer Coding Projects for Kids, Carol Vorderman (DK Children, 2019)

Incredible Robots in Space (Incredible Robots), Louise and Richard Spilsbury (Raintree, 2017)

Robot: Meet the Machines of the Future, Laura Buller, Clive Gifford and Andrea Mills (DK Children, 2018)

WEBSITES

www.bbc.co.uk/newsround/43365076
Watch the football playing robots in action!

www.dkfindout.com/uk/computer-coding/what-is-coding
Find out more about computer coding.

INDEX